We Share in the Eucharist

Jesus walks with you as you prepare to celebrate your First Communion. He loves you and wants you to share the Bread of Life.

AUTHORS
Francoise Darcy-Berube and Jean-Paul Berube

EDITORS, NEW EDITION
Gwen Costello and Myrtle Power

On Our Way with Jesus, *New Edition*

Sacramental Preparation Resources

We Prepare for Reconciliation
We Share in the Eucharist

Nihil Obstat
Caroline Altpeter IBVM
Archdiocese of Toronto
19 June 2009

Imprimatur
+Thomas Collins
Archbishop of Toronto
1 July 2009

Liturgical Advisor: Rev. William Burke, Director, National Liturgy Office
(English Sector), Canadian Conference of Catholic Bishops

© 2012 Novalis Publishing Inc.

Cover: Anna Payne-Krzyzanowski

Design & Layout: Sarah Orr, ArtPlus

Art Direction: Donna Guilfoyle, ArtPlus

Illustrations: ArtPlus: pp. 4, 5, 25, 33, 36; June Bradford: pp. 11,16, 18, 29, 34, 35, 37, 38, 45, 47, 52, 56 and Prayer Book art; Heather Collins: pp. 15, 28, 30, 35, 42, 43, 48, 49; Vesna Krstanovic: p.13; Suzanne Mogensen: pp. 12, 20, 36, 40, 46; Anna Payne-Krzyzanowski: pp. 4, 5, 7, 8, 14, 15, 19, 20-24, 26, 27, 31, 39, 41, 51, 53, and icons.

Photo credits: Page 3: © iStockphoto.com/stray_cat; Page 6: © iStockphoto.com/Legacy One Photography; Page 9: © WP Wittman Photography; Page 14: © WP Wittman Photography; Page 16: © WP Wittman Photography; Page 25: © WP Wittman Photography; Page 26: Right: © WP Wittman Photography; Page 26: Left: © WP Wittman Photography; Page 30: 2009 © Tammy McAllister. Image from BigStockPhoto.com; Page 31: top right: © WP Wittman Photography; Page 31: bottom left: © WP Wittman Photography; Page 32: right: © WP Wittman Photography; Page 32: left: © WP Wittman Photography; Page 33: © WP Wittman Photography; Page 44: © WP Wittman Photography; Page 50: top left: © WP Wittman Photography; Page 50: bottom centre: © WP Wittman Photography; Page 52: © WP Wittman Photography; Page 53: top right: © Juriah Mosin/Shutterstock; Page 53: bottom right: © iStockphoto.com/peanut8481; Page 54: © WP Wittman Photography; Page 55: © WP Wittman Photography

Publishing Office:
Novalis
10 Lower Spadina Ave., Suite 400
Toronto, ON, Canada
M5V 2Z2

Tel: 416-363-3303 Toll-Free: 1-877-702-7773
Fax: 416-363-9409 Toll-Free: 1-877-702-7775
E-mail: resources@novalis.ca
www.novalis.ca

Head Office:
4475 Frontenac Street
Montreal, QC, Canada
H2H 2S2

ISBN: 978-2-89646-462-3 (Novalis)
Cataloguing in Publication is available from Library and Archives Canada.

We acknowledge the financial support of the Government of Canada through the Canada Book Fund for business development activities.

Published in the United States by
Twenty-Third Publications
A Division of Bayard
One Montauk Ave., Suite 200
P.O. Box 6015
New London, CT 06320
Tel: 860-437-3012 Toll-Free: 1-800-321-0411
E-mail: ttpubs@aol.com
www.23rdpublications.com

ISBN: 978-1-58595-745-3 (Twenty-Third Publications)
Library of Congress Catalog Card Number: 2009933794

Printed in Canada

5 4 3 2   15 14 13 12 11

Table of Contents

A Special Invitation

Dear Child,

Imagine how you would feel if a famous person, someone you really admire, invited you to be a guest of honour at a huge party!

Well, guess what? You HAVE been chosen to be a guest at a wonderful celebration.

And the one inviting you is Jesus.

As you begin to prepare for your First Communion day, Jesus will be walking beside you all along the way, just as he has done since your baptism.

When you are ready, there will be a great celebration in your parish where you will be welcomed to the Table of the Lord by the whole parish community. You will be the guest of Jesus himself.

If you are ready to begin, just sign your name below.

My First Communion

I will celebrate my First Communion on

.... at

(Date)

....

(Name of my church)

....

(My pastor's name)   (My teacher's name)

A memory of my
special day

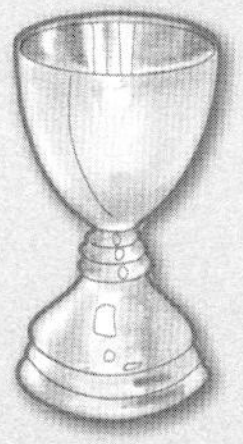

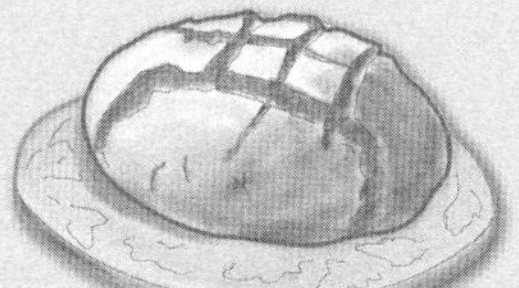

Signatures of people who helped me prepare
for my First Communion

....

....

....

From the Liturgy

Father, because you love us, you invite us to come to your table.

—Eucharistic Prayer I for Children

Belen's parents work hard to earn money, so they try to spend it carefully. But Belen will soon be eight years old and that will be a very special occasion. Her parents decide to have a surprise party for her. They invite Belen's closest friends.

What Do You Think?

- **What other days do you celebrate besides birthdays?**

. . . .

- **Which celebrations mean the most to your family?**

. . . .

- **What is your favourite way to celebrate?**

. . . .

Her father knows a magician who will show up right in the middle of the party.

Can you imagine the excitement when he arrives? Belen's parents believe that family celebrations are very important.

Your family celebrates special occasions. So does your church family. It celebrates feast days like Christmas and Easter and special occasions like your baptism and First Communion.

A Day to Remember

After Jesus died on the cross, Peter, Andrew, and all the followers of Jesus gathered together. They were very sad. Jesus was their best friend. He taught them about God's Law of Love and showed them how to live it.

Suddenly, some women ran into the room. Early that morning, before sunrise, they had gone to the tomb where Jesus was buried. Now they had some incredible news.

The tomb was empty! Then the words of Jesus came back to them: "On the third day, I will rise again." They were so happy! Jesus had risen, just as he had said.

Imagine yourself in the place of Peter. He was sad when Jesus died on the cross, but now was filled with joy. Can you remember a time when you were so happy you could hardly speak? It must have been like that for Peter and the others.

It's terrible — just terrible!

What will we do without Jesus?

The tomb is open... the body of Jesus is gone!

What? We have to go see for ourselves.

He is risen. Alleluia! Alleluia!

A Meal to Remember

A new life began for the friends of Jesus. Jesus had died on the cross, but God raised him to new life. His friends often talked together about all that Jesus had done and said. They remembered his last meal with them, and his beautiful words came back to them.

Imagine yourself at the table with Jesus and his friends. Put yourself in the picture below. What would you have said to Jesus about his incredible words? What do you think he meant?

. . . .

. . . .

. . . .

The Church Teaches...

Jesus is really and truly present in Communion. He gives us his body and blood.

—adapted for children from Catechism of the Catholic Church (CCC) #1375

At the end of the meal, Jesus said: "Do this in memory of me." From then on, when his followers shared the bread and wine, they remembered Jesus, and he was there with them.

Just as Jesus asked, his followers soon began to gather every Sunday, the day of the resurrection, in memory of him. For them, every Sunday was like celebrating Easter all over again.

At first his followers met in homes around a dinner table. But soon there were too many of them. They had to move to larger spaces. As the number of followers grew, they built churches where they could share their faith and love in memory of Jesus.

Your Parish Church

The people in your parish, which is also called a Christian community,
gather every Sunday just as Christians have done since the time of Jesus.
When you celebrate Mass with your parish family, Jesus is truly there with you.
Your parish church is the place where you will celebrate your First Communion.

Can you answer these questions?

HINT: Ask your parents or teacher for help.

✝ What is the name of your parish?

. . . .

✝ Why do you think it has that name?

. . . .

✝ Who is the leader in your parish?

. . . .

✝ Who are some of the people who work with your pastor?

. . . .

. . . .

Draw or write here about what you
like best in your parish church.

See how well you have listened and learned. Use these words to answer the questions below: **Communion, memory, Sunday, Mass, Jesus, Easter**

1. _ _ _ _ _ _ is the greatest Christian feast day.

2. It is the day God raised _ _ _ _ _ to new life.

3. During his last meal, Jesus said: "Do this in _ _ _ _ _ _ of me."

4. After the Resurrection, the friends of Jesus began to meet on _ _ _ _ _ _.

5. At _ _ _ _, the members of your parish family share the Bread of Life.

6. When you celebrate your First _ _ _ _ _ _ _ _ _ _, you will also share the Bread of Life.

From the Bible

Jesus taught his followers God's Law of Love. Here is how the Bible describes it: "You shall love the Lord your God with all your heart, and with all your soul, and with all your might."

—Deuteronomy 6:5

At the Last Supper, Jesus taught his followers this new law of love: "Love one another as I have loved you."

—adapted from John 15:12

Let Us Pray

Invite your family to say this prayer before meals with you:

Lord Jesus, bless this meal that we are about to share, and please bless all the people in our world who are hungry this day. Amen.

2 We Learn about the Mass

This book is called the Lectionary.

When you go to Mass, also called the celebration of the Lord's Supper, or the celebration of the Eucharist, you look, you listen, you sing, and you make gestures. You watch what the priest does as he leads the people in prayer. But it is *all of us together* who celebrate the Eucharist. The two main parts of the Mass are the **Liturgy of the Word** and the **Liturgy of the Eucharist.**

The Parts of the Mass

The Gathering
- The people arrive, greet one another, and gather in response to God's call
- The priest enters with servers and other ministers and everyone sings
- The priest greets all of us gathered to share the Lord's Supper
- We then pray for forgiveness and we praise God

The Liturgy of the Word
- We listen to the Word of God
- The priest speaks to us to help us better understand the Word of God
- We profess our faith
- We pray for the whole world

The Liturgy of the Eucharist
- We give thanks to God
- We remember the words of Jesus
- We share the Bread of Life and the Cup of his Blood

The Farewell
- The priest blesses us and asks us to love and serve one another
- The priest and others leave in procession and everyone sings

Things We See at Mass

The next time you go to Mass, look for the things Father Joseph is showing Sasha, Olivia, and Paulo. All these things are used for the celebration of the Lord's Supper.

Father Joseph also told them about the other things on the altar. Here's what he said:

> The altar is the table for the Lord's Supper, so it's a very special table. The candles are a sign that Jesus, our light, is with us.

The large prayer book on the altar is called the **Missal**. It contains all the Mass prayers. The second book used at Mass is called the **Lectionary**. (See the Lectionary on page 12.) The Lectionary contains all the readings from the Bible. The priest uses a small gold plate, called the **paten** (PAT-en), and a cup with a lid, called the **ciborium** (sah-BORE-ee-um), to hold the hosts or communion bread. The other cup, the **chalice** (CHAL-ess), holds the wine.

Father Joseph told the children not to worry if they couldn't remember these "church" names. "The important thing to know," he said, "is that they are used for a very special meal: the Lord's Supper."

We Share Greetings

Did You Know?

▸ You are invited to say the Mass prayers in a loud, clear voice.

▸ The Mass has been the special prayer of Christians for two thousand years.

▸ It is a custom in the Church for the priest to wear special garments called vestments at Mass.

▸ Several times during Mass the priest says, "The Lord be with you." What do you answer? (Check your answer at the bottom of the page.)

When you enter the church, the priest or other greeters say hello to you to make you feel welcome. People greet one another as they gather. You should also greet those around you before Mass begins.

At the beginning of Mass, the priest greets everyone from the altar, saying:

The grace of our Lord Jesus Christ, and the love of God, and the communion of the Holy Spirit be with you all.

Everyone answers:

And with your spirit.

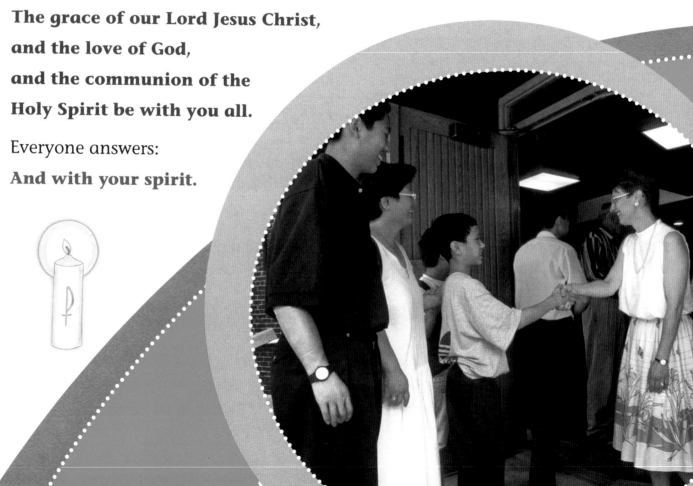

ANSWER: And with your spirit.

We Are a Family

When we come to Mass, we join Catholics all over the world in worship. We sing, we make gestures, we stand and kneel. We pray the same prayers in many different languages. We ask God to take care of the poor and the suffering. We all gather in memory of Jesus. How lucky we are to be called to the Lord's Table!

The Church Teaches...

At Mass we share our faith in the real presence of Christ.

—adapted for children from CCC #1382

Let Us Pray

Praise God with shouts of joy, all people! Sing to the glory of God's name.

—adapted from Psalm 42:4

We Ask Forgiveness

Once upon a time, there was a little prince who came from a faraway planet. One day he met a very wise fox in the desert. The fox explained to the little prince that before you meet a friend, you must "dress up your heart."

• • • • • • • • • •

This is just what you do at Mass before meeting the Lord. You quiet your heart and ask yourself, "Have I dressed up my heart by praying, doing good for others, and giving up my bad habits?"

The priest says: **Brothers and sisters, let us acknowledge our sins, and so prepare ourselves to celebrate the sacred mysteries.**

The people remain silent for a few moments and then praise God for the gift of forgiveness by chanting these words: **Lord, have mercy. Christ, have mercy. Lord, have mercy.**

In Greek, the words are *Kyrie, Eleison* (keer-ee-AY a-LAY-ee-sahn) and *Christe, Eleison* (kris-TAY a-LAY-ee-sahn).

Sometimes parishes use these words in the chant. When you say them you are speaking a little Greek!

Then the priest says: **May almighty God have mercy on us, forgive us our sins, and bring us into everlasting life.**

We answer: **Amen!**

We Sing Our Praise

After God gives us the gift of forgiveness, we proclaim the greatness of God by singing "Glory to God." This is what the angels sang when Jesus was born.

After this song of praise, the priest prays the Opening Prayer. He asks God to be with us and open our hearts. At the end of the prayer we again answer: **Amen!**

The first part of the Mass is now over.

Did You Know?

▸ **During Mass we "dress up our hearts" because we are meeting Jesus, our best friend.**

▸ **At home, you can make a prayer corner, a space where you can pray. You can keep a Bible, a rosary, and special pictures in your prayer corner.**

▸ **Jesus is always with you, morning, noon, and night.**

Read this prayer slowly and then fill the space with happy colours. Make a colourful frame to go around the prayer.

Glory to God in the highest,
and on earth peace to people of good will.
We praise you, we bless you,
we adore you, we glorify you,
we give you thanks for your great glory,
Lord God, heavenly King,
O God, almighty Father.
Lord Jesus Christ, Only Begotten Son,
Lord God, Lamb of God,
Son of the Father,
you take away the sins of the world, have mercy on us;
you take away the sins of the world, receive our prayer;
you are seated at the right hand of the Father,
have mercy on us.
For you alone are the Holy One,
you alone are the Lord,
you alone are the Most High, Jesus Christ,
with the Holy Spirit,
in the glory of God the Father.
Amen.

Words to Remember...

Liturgy ~ the "official" prayer of the Church that all Catholics share

Lectionary ~ the book that contains the readings for Mass

Have mercy ~ another way to say, "Please forgive me."

Amen ~ a word we say in prayer that means "Yes, I do believe it."

From the Liturgy

God, our loving Father, we are glad to give you thanks and praise because you love us. With Jesus we sing your praise.

—Eucharistic Prayer II for Children

True or False?

1. At Mass we gather with other Catholics in our parish and all over the world. _____

2. The priest wears special garments called robes. _____

3. "Amen" means I do NOT believe. _____

4. To "dress up your heart" means to wear your best clothes. _____

5. The Mass begins with a special greeting. _____

6. At the beginning of Mass, we give praise and thanks for God's love and forgiveness. _____

7. The altar is the book the priest reads from at Mass. _____

Let Us Pray

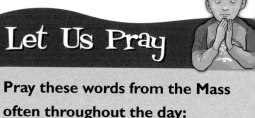

Pray these words from the Mass often throughout the day:

Lord, have mercy.
Christ, have mercy.
Lord, have mercy.

At Mass, a person called a **lector** or **reader** proclaims words from the Bible. The Bible is a very special book that tells about God's great love for us. It also tells about people who lived long ago and who had great faith in God. When we read or hear stories from the Bible, we are learning the history of Jesus. This history also becomes our story because we are the followers of Jesus.

PEOPLE OF FAITH GALLERY

We Learn about the Bible

Some of the people you saw in the People of Faith Gallery were leaders of the Jewish people. They were ancestors of Jesus, and he learned about them as a child. When you read the Bible, you can learn about them, too. Here is part of the story.

• • • • • • • • • • •

At the time of Abraham, people believed in many different gods and worshipped them all. But God asked Abraham to be the father of a new people who would worship the one true God. Abraham moved to a new land as God asked. There he and his wife, Sarah, had a son named Isaac. Abraham followed the paths of God. He spoke to God as a friend. He taught Isaac to do the same.

Later, some of Isaac's children and grandchildren moved to the land of Egypt where they could get food. But after many years, the leader there decided to make them slaves. Their lives were very hard. Then God called Moses to lead the people out of Egypt back to their own land. Moses did as God asked, but it took 40 years for the people to return home. During that time, God gave Moses this Law of Love:

"You shall love the Lord your God with all your heart, and with all your soul, and with all your might."

—Deuteronomy 6:5

When Jesus' ancestors arrived back in their land, they formed a kingdom to keep order. Their leader was King David. Like Abraham and Moses, David taught his people to love and serve one God. To tell God of his faith and love, David wrote beautiful prayers that we call the **psalms.** We sing one of the psalms every Sunday at Mass.

When the people forgot about God, others, called **prophets**, reminded them to turn back to God. The prophet Isaiah made this important announcement:

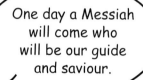

One day a Messiah will come who will be our guide and saviour.

Prepare your hearts. Someone greater than I am is coming to save you.

Then came John the Baptist, the cousin of Jesus. He prepared the way for Jesus.

We Welcome Jesus

Jesus was the great one John the Baptist spoke about. When Jesus grew up, he talked about God's Law of Love to all the people of his land.

Jesus helped the sick, welcomed children, and forgave sinners. On the night before he died, he gave his friends the Bread of Life.

Jesus taught God's Law of Love everywhere he went. The leaders became jealous. People were following Jesus and not them. They arrested him and nailed him to a cross. Before he died, he did something amazing. He forgave his enemies.

Then, on the third day, God raised Jesus to new life.

The Father loves you. Love one another.

This is my body and blood, given for you.

Father, forgive them.

The Lord is risen! Praise God.

From the Liturgy

Loving Father, we remember that Jesus died and rose again to save the world.

—Eucharistic Prayer II for Children

After his resurrection, Jesus appeared several times to his friends. They were amazed and filled with joy. Jesus told them he was returning to his Father. Before he left, he asked them to share God's Law of Love with everyone. Then he promised to send them the Holy Spirit.

As Jesus' followers and his mother waited for the Spirit, they were praying together. Suddenly a great gust of wind filled the house. Flashes of fire touched each one of them but did not burn them.

They were all filled with the Holy Spirit. The Holy Spirit gave them courage. Peter and the others began at once to spread the news about Jesus. They told everyone: "Love one another as Jesus loved you."

A few years later, a man named Saul was on his way to arrest everyone who believed in Jesus. On the road to Damascus, Saul met the risen Christ. From that moment on, Saul became a follower. He changed his name to Paul and became a great missionary, spreading the news about Jesus everywhere he went.

The Church Teaches...

Be merciful and forgiving, as Jesus was, and love others as he has loved us.

—adapted for children from CCC #2842

O Lord Jesus, be with me as I share the gospel with others.

The Liturgy of the Word

In the first two readings, we listen to the messages of the prophets and apostles. They tell us about God and teach us to follow God's Law of Love. At the end of each reading, the reader says:

The word of the Lord.

All answer:

Thanks be to God.

After the first reading, we sing one of the psalms.

Then we stand to listen to the gospel. But before it is read, we express our joy by singing, **Alleluia!** which means "Praise the Lord."

The Lord is compassionate and gracious, slow to anger, abounding in love.

—adapted from Psalm 103:8

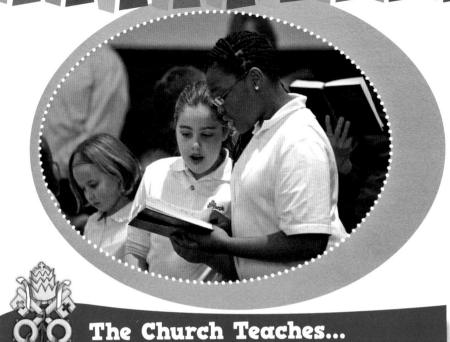

The Church Teaches...

The Liturgy of the Word includes the writings of the prophets and the memoirs of the apostles.

—adapted for children from CCC #1349

Did You Know?

▶ The word **Gospel** means "good news."

▶ The Gospels contain the teachings of Jesus.

▶ There are four Gospels.

▶ The Gospels are named after their writers: Matthew, Mark, Luke, and John.

We Hear the Gospel

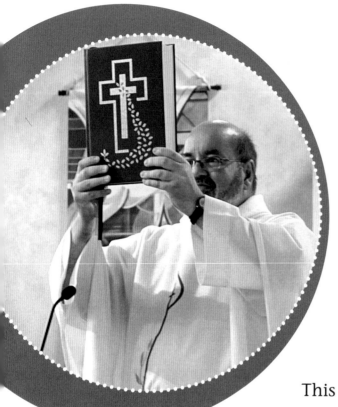

Before he reads the gospel, the priest or deacon says: **The Lord be with you.**

All answer: **And with your spirit.**

Then he says: **A reading from the holy Gospel according to (Matthew, Mark, Luke, or John).**

All answer: **Glory to you, O Lord.**

People make the sign of the cross on their forehead, lips, and heart at this time.

This is a sign of respect for the gospel and a way of saying, "I love your Word, O God. I want to remember it, to speak it, and to keep it in my heart."

The gospel tells a story about Jesus, or shares something he taught. After reading it, the priest or deacon says: **The Gospel of the Lord.**

All answer: **Praise to you, Lord Jesus Christ.**

Then the priest or deacon speaks to us to help us better understand the Word of God. This is called the **homily**.

We Profess Our Faith

Every Sunday after the homily, we name all the things we believe as Christians. The words we use are from the Creed. The word **Creed** means "beliefs." There are two Creeds that can be used during Mass. The longer one is called the **Nicene Creed**. The other is called the **Apostles' Creed**.

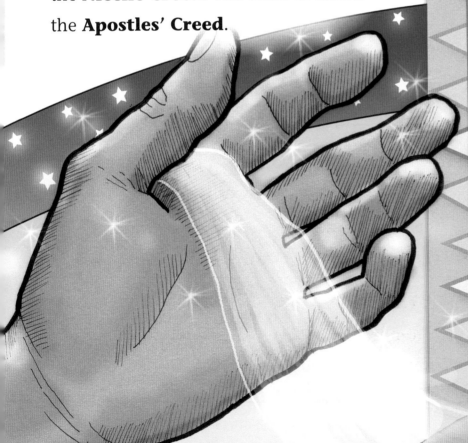

The Apostles' Creed

I believe in God, the Father almighty,
   Creator of heaven and earth,
and in Jesus Christ, his only Son, our Lord,*
   who was conceived by the Holy Spirit,
   born of the Virgin Mary,
   suffered under Pontius Pilate,
   was crucified, died and was buried;
   he descended into hell;
   on the third day he rose again from the dead;
   he ascended into heaven,
   and is seated at the right hand of God
      the Father almighty;
   from there he will come to judge the living and the dead.
I believe in the Holy Spirit,
   the holy catholic Church,
   the communion of saints,
   the forgiveness of sins,
   the resurrection of the body,
   and life everlasting. Amen.

* *We bow at the next two lines.*

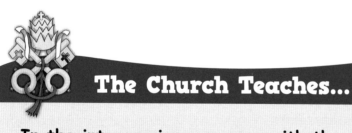

Did You Know?

The word **intercession** means to pray for another person or situation. If you could add an intercession at Mass, what would you pray for?

I would pray for . . . .

. . . .

and also for . . . .

. . . .

The Church Teaches...

In the intercessions we pray with the whole Church in heaven and on earth.

—adapted for children from CCC #1354

We Pray for Others

People all over the world are God's children. That is why we pray for one another and for the entire human family every week at Mass. These prayers are called **Intercessory Prayers** or **Prayers of the Faithful.** During these prayers, we think of what is happening in our world and in our own country. We pray for our Church leaders, for our country's leaders, for the hungry, for the sick, for countries at war, and for all who are suffering in any way. We also pray for those who have died. We ask for the courage to help one another make our world better for all.

The reader prays these prayers and we all answer:
Lord, hear our prayer.

This is the end of the Liturgy of the Word.

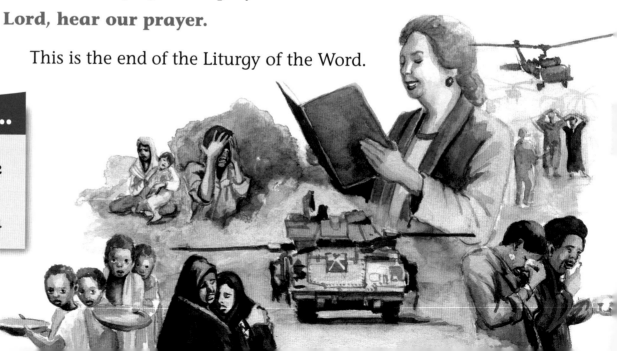

So far, you have learned about the greetings we share at Mass and about the Liturgy of the Word. See if you can finish these sentences:

1. At Mass, we share the W_ _ _ of God.

2. The B_ _ _ _ tells us the great story of God's love for all people.

3. For Christians, the coming of J _ _ _ _ _, his death, and his resurrection are the most important events in this story.

4. With the H _ _ _ _ S _ _ _ _ _ _ _ guiding us, we continue to live God's story.

Words to Remember...

Lector ~ person who proclaims words from the Bible at Mass

Psalms ~ prayers from the Bible inspired by King David

Prophets ~ special people who announce God's Law of Love

Alleluia ~ a word that means "praise God"

Homily ~ a talk about God's Word given by the priest or deacon at Mass

Creed ~ beliefs

Intercessory Prayers ~ prayers for all the human family

From the Liturgy

Learn these words by heart and say them often. "Lord, you are holy; you are kind to us and to all. For this we thank you."

—Eucharistic Prayer III for Children (adapted)

When the priest greets you at Mass saying, "The Lord be with you," what do you answer?

....

Alicia and Kieran's grandmother bakes her own bread. She knows that Alicia and Kieran love to eat it fresh out of the oven.

What a treat! Thanks for baking this for us.

Ooh, strawberry jam, too. Thanks, Grandma. It's delicious!

While they were eating, Grandma told them how bread is made and how much work and time it takes from start to finish. The farmer plants wheat. When it is grown, the farmer collects the grain and takes it to the mill. There it is ground into flour. Grandma uses the flour to make the bread dough.

Jesus chose bread and wine to give himself to us at Communion because bread and wine are sources of life and joy. Bread satisfies our hunger. Wine lifts our spirits.

Before the bread and wine are carried to the altar, there is an offertory collection.

People put money in the baskets to help support the work and needs of the parish.

From the beginning, the Church has used some of this money to help people in need.

We Offer Bread and Wine

After the gifts are carried to the altar, the priest says these two beautiful prayers, one offering the bread, the other offering the wine.

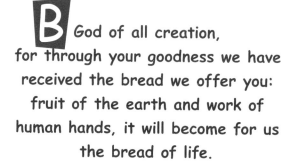

lessed are you, Lord

B God of all creation,
for through your goodness we have
received the bread we offer you:
fruit of the earth and work of
human hands, it will become for us
the bread of life.

All answer: Blessed be God for ever!

B lessed are you, Lord
God of all creation,
for through your goodness we have
received the wine we offer you:
fruit of the vine and work of human
hands, it will become our
spiritual drink.

All answer: Blessed be God for ever!

What Do You Think?

- **Have you ever been chosen for the Presentation of the Gifts? What did you carry?** . . . .

- **What do we mean when we pray "blessed are you" to God?**

. . . .

We Share in the Eucharist

With the prayers from the revised Roman Missal

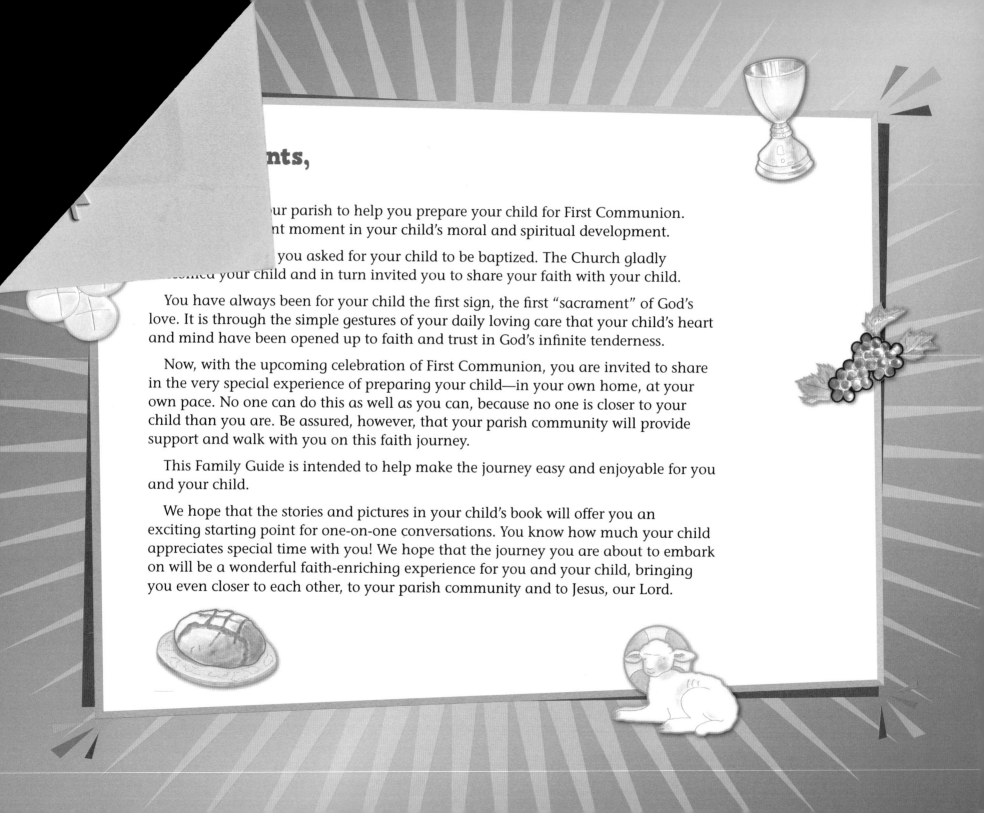

nts,

...ur parish to help you prepare your child for First Communion. ...nt moment in your child's moral and spiritual development.

... you asked for your child to be baptized. The Church gladly ...ed your child and in turn invited you to share your faith with your child.

You have always been for your child the first sign, the first "sacrament" of God's love. It is through the simple gestures of your daily loving care that your child's heart and mind have been opened up to faith and trust in God's infinite tenderness.

Now, with the upcoming celebration of First Communion, you are invited to share in the very special experience of preparing your child—in your own home, at your own pace. No one can do this as well as you can, because no one is closer to your child than you are. Be assured, however, that your parish community will provide support and walk with you on this faith journey.

This Family Guide is intended to help make the journey easy and enjoyable for you and your child.

We hope that the stories and pictures in your child's book will offer you an exciting starting point for one-on-one conversations. You know how much your child appreciates special time with you! We hope that the journey you are about to embark on will be a wonderful faith-enriching experience for you and your child, bringing you even closer to each other, to your parish community and to Jesus, our Lord.

Your Role

As you prepare your child for the sacrament of First Communion (also called First Eucharist), you will

- help them discover that Jesus shows them the way to God
- encourage them to develop simple habits of prayer that will sustain their spiritual life while strengthening their character
- lead them gradually to fuller participation at Sunday Mass by helping them learn the meaning of the rites and rituals and pray with Bible words
- instill in them a deep desire to encounter Jesus often in the sacrament of Eucharist.

Our approach

This preparation journey is built on two very important foundations.

1 **Regular conversations with your child**

Spend one-on-one time discussing and reinforcing what your child is learning. It's easy! Just read a few pages together from your child's book and use the ideas provided to begin your conversations. After reading and talking, do the suggested activities together.

Good conversations happen in an atmosphere of joy, peace, and prayer. Here are a few ways to create such a mood at home.

- Talk to your child and agree on the best time for your conversations. Stick to the schedule as best you can.
- Choose a place where you won't be disturbed, and ask other family members to give you some privacy.
- Before you begin, light a candle or vigil light to create a prayerful atmosphere. Share a moment of silence together to become aware of God's presence. Then pray a short prayer, such as: "Dear God, be with us as we talk" or "Give us your joy and love, dear God."

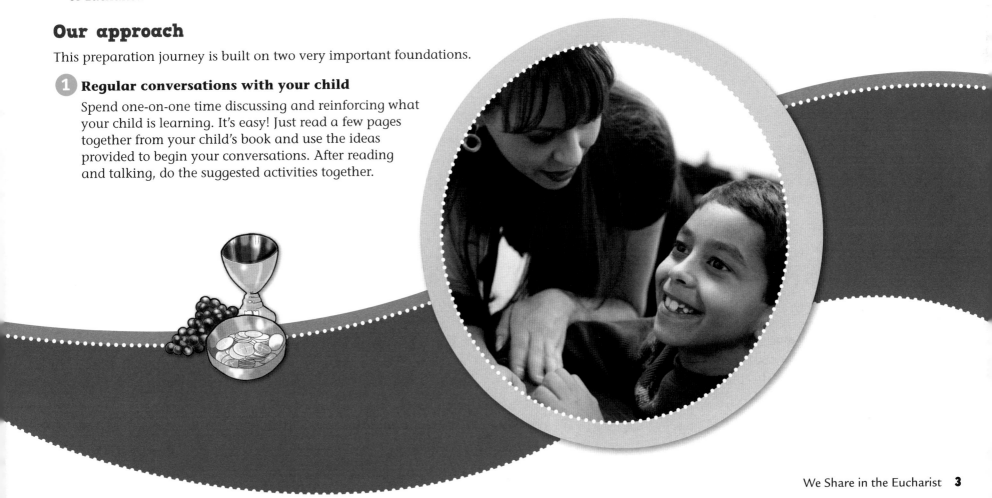

② Special attention to your child's daily life and prayer

This journey of preparing for First Communion is an intense time. Your child will learn what it means to be a Christian, a follower of Jesus Christ. You will want to be extra attentive to your child's attitude and participation at Mass so you can discuss it and reflect on it together. Encourage your child to put into practice what he or she discovers at each step on this journey.

This journey also offers a good opportunity to develop the habit of daily prayer, which is important for your child's whole life. At the centre of this guide you will find six prayer cards, one for each of the six themes in your child's book. Set aside some prayer time each day. (Remember: this means praying with your child, not just listening to your child's prayers.) Cut out the prayers and give one to your child at the beginning of each theme. Read the prayers together morning and evening. You may wish to invite other family members to join you. Help your child set up his or her prayer corner: a space where he or she can pray with some privacy. In the prayer corner, place a Bible, a picture of Jesus or pictures your child has drawn, and a candle. Add other objects as your child continues on this journey of preparation.

At the back of your child's book you will find a cut-out book of prayers based on the prayers of the Mass (plus several traditional church prayers). Help your child cut out and assemble his or her personal prayer book. Say one of the prayers in "My Prayer Book" together at meal prayers with your family so that your child will come to memorize them and use them for his or her daily prayer.

Celebrating the start of the journey

Once your child begins this journey, have a meal to celebrate. Invite grandparents, godparents, and close friends from the parish. Serve a special dessert. During the meal, give your child a card signed by all present with thoughts and blessings for a "happy journey to First Communion." Take time at this meal to tell family members that you will be having regular private conversations with your child as he or she prepares.

(Ideally, both parents will be part of this journey and will be involved as much as possible throughout the year.)

Preparing for each theme

There are six themes (or chapters) in your child's book. Before starting a new theme, take time to read everything related to that theme in your child's book and in this Family Guide. The themes flow from one to the next in order. The points made in each theme are important to what follows, so make sure you do each one.

Now it's time to get started!

Goals

- to encourage you and your child to focus on the importance of family meals and celebrations
- to awaken in your child's heart the joy of being invited to Sunday Mass
- to help your child discover the meaning of Sunday for the Christian community

Parent/child conversations

Pages 4 and 5 *(These page numbers and the pages that follow under "Parent/child conversations" refer to the pages in your child's book.)*

- Set a prayerful, peaceful tone for your first conversation. This will set the tone for all the others. Take time to get settled. Invite your child to light the candle. Share a moment of silence to become aware of God's presence.
- Read the letter on page 4 of your child's book. Talk about how it feels to be "chosen" by someone important. Talk about why Jesus is such a special person. For example: he taught people about God's Law of Love; he healed the sick; he prayed every day; he was kind to the poor. Explain that Jesus first chose your child at baptism. Be sure your child understands that he or she is preparing for First Communion before signing page 4.

Pages 6 and 7

- Read about Belen's birthday party on page 6. Have your child answer the "What Do You Think?" questions. Share your answers as well.
- Now read the story about Peter and the other followers on page 7. Talk about what Peter must have felt. Ask your child: If you had been there, what would you have said to Peter? How do you think you would have felt?

Pages 8, 9 and 10

- Read pages 8 and 9 together. Talk about memories. What is it like to remember someone? The friends of Jesus remembered the Last Supper and the words that Jesus said. They remembered him by gathering every Sunday to share the bread and wine. Explain that after First Communion, your child can also share in the Eucharist at Mass.
- Read "The Church Teaches" on page 9 with your child. Have him or her repeat it after you. (Note: children do not usually question how or why Jesus would give his body and blood as food. Because this is a mystery of our faith, that Jesus is really present in the Eucharist, we believe it. Assure your child that when we share Jesus' body and blood in communion, we are saying "yes" to Jesus and his teachings, and "yes" to all that he asks of us.)
- Talk about the questions on page 10. What did your child write or draw within the church?
- End this conversation by praying together this prayer: *Jesus, we say "amen" to you; we say "yes" to you. Be with us today in everything we do.*

Page 11

- Help your child fill in the blanks. Be sure he or she can define the words *Eucharist, memory, Sunday, Mass,* and *Jesus,* at least in simple terms.
- Read the "From the Bible" verses together. Talk about what they mean to your child.
- Close by offering your child a simple blessing. Trace the sign of the cross with your thumb on his or her forehead as you say, "May God bless you as you prepare for First Communion."

2 We Learn about the Mass

Goals

- **to help your child understand the Mass better: how it unfolds and what objects are used**
- **to focus on the spiritual attitudes we need to participate fully**
- **to awaken in your child the desire to prepare well for meeting the Lord in the celebration of the Eucharist**

Parent/child conversations

Pages 12, 13, and 14

- Read together and talk about the chart on page 12.
- Review some of the things Father Joseph is showing the children on page 13. (Your child does not need to remember these "church words." The aim is to know that these things are used for a very special meal, the Lord's Supper, and perhaps to look for them when your family goes to Mass.)
- Read the "Did You Know?" statements on page 14. Then say to your child, "The Lord be with you." Have him or her answer, "And with your spirit."

Pages 15 and 16

- Look at the picture on page 15. Talk about it with your child, then read the section that begins with "When we come to Mass."
- If possible, borrow *The Little Prince* (by Antoine de Saint-Exupéry) from the library and look through it together. Show your child the pictures of the prince and the fox on page 16 of the child's book. Does your child understand the concept of "dressing up your heart"? Talk about how we can prepare to meet Jesus at Mass. (We can prepare by getting to Mass on time, saying the responses to prayers, singing, and praying. Your own example will help your child learn good habits.)
- End by folding your hands and praying this prayer together: *Lord, have mercy; Christ, have mercy; Lord, have mercy.*

Pages 17 and 18

- Remind your child that the "Glory to God" we pray at Mass was the prayer of the angels when Jesus was born. Say each line of the prayer, and have your child say it after you. Then discuss the "Did You Know?" statements on page 17.
- Talk about the "True or False?" statements on page 18. If any of them confuse your child, discuss the answers together. For example, the garments the priest wears are called "vestments," not robes, although they do look like robes.
- Read the "Words to Remember." Be sure your child can define them in his or her own words.
- Pray together the "From the Liturgy" prayer. Invite your child to then pray silently for all the things he or she is grateful for. You can do this as well. Afterwards, discuss what you prayed for. Close by making a sign of the cross on your child's forehead.

God Gives Us Life

In the Morning

Parent: Remember, Jesus walks with us always. Here is his message for us today.

(If you have a family Bible, show it to your child before reading this verse, to help him or her recognize these as special words: God's Word.)

> You shall love the Lord your God
> with all your heart,
> and with all your soul,
> and with all your mind...
> and you shall love your neighbour as yourself.
>
> —Matthew 22:34-39

Child: Thank you, loving God, for teaching me your Law of Love through Jesus.

Parent: Jesus will be with us today in all we do.

Child: Thank you, Jesus, for watching over me.

Parent: Let us now share the sign of our faith ...

Parent/Child: In the name of the Father, and of the Son, and of the Holy Spirit. Amen.

In the Evening

Parent: Let us remember that Jesus has been with us today as we tried to practise God's Law of Love. Let us listen to his message for us this evening.

> This is my commandment,
> that you love one another as I have loved you.
>
> —John 15:12

Child: Dear God, thank you for loving me so much.

Parent: Your Son, Jesus, asks us to love others as much as he loves us. We need your help to do this. So together we pray,

Parent/Child: Help us, dear God, to love as you do. Watch over us now and all night long. Amen.

(Now trace the sign of the cross on your child's forehead.)

In the Morning

Parent: Remember that Jesus will be with us this day. Let us listen together to his Word and keep it in our hearts.

"Let the little children come to me, and do not stop them; for it is to such as these that the kingdom of heaven belongs." And then he laid his hands on them and [blessed them].

—Matthew 19:14

Child: Dear Jesus, thank you for blessing the children. Thank you for blessing me.

Parent: Bless my child today, Jesus, in all that he/she does.

Child: Help me to think of you often today.

Parent: Let us praise God together as we begin our day …

Parent/Child: We are filled with wonder and praise, O God, when we see what you do for us through Jesus your Son. Amen.

In the Evening

Parent: Let us take time now to talk to God before we go to sleep. *(Pause for a few seconds)* God is with us at all times and blesses us this evening …

May the grace of our Lord Jesus Christ, and the love of God, and the communion of the Holy Spirit be with you.

Child: Thank you, God, for your blessing this night.

Parent: Lord, watch over us and fill us with your grace.

Child: Thank you, God, for putting your love in my heart.

Parent: Let us now pray to God our Father …

Parent/Child: God, our loving Father, we are glad to give you thanks and praise because you love us. With Jesus we sing your praise. Holy, holy, holy are you, now and forever.

(Now trace the sign of the cross on your child's forehead.)

We Share God's Word

In the Morning

Parent: Remember that God fills our hearts with joy. Here is God's Word for us today.

> The Lord is merciful and gracious,
> slow to anger, and abounding in steadfast love.
>
> —Psalm 103:8

Child: Dear God, fill my heart with your love and care.

Parent: Let us pray together that God will walk with us in all we do today. May we care for others as God cares for us.

Child: Dear God, I will try to treat everyone well today.

Parent: On this new day of life, we thank God for all our gifts and graces.

Parent/Child: O God, you are so kind and good.
May we live this day, just as we should.
Guide us, help us, show us the way.
Thank you for giving us this day.
Amen.

In the Evening

Parent: Thank you, God, for your goodness and love this day. Thank you for your words in the Bible that teach and guide us.

> We love your Word, O God.
> We want to remember it, to speak it,
> and to keep it in our hearts.

(Make a small cross on your forehead, your lips, and over your heart as you pray these words. Invite your child to do the same.)

Parent: Let us now talk to God about our day, what gave us joy and what was difficult.

(Pause for a few seconds)

Parent/Child: You have been with us in everything we did today. Thank you, God. Amen.

(Now trace the sign of the cross on your child's forehead.)

We Give Thanks

In the Morning

Parent: Remember today that Jesus is with us. Let us give thanks together.

Parent/Child: Lord, you are holy; you are kind to us and to all. For this we thank you.

Child: Dear and loving God, help me to say "thank you" often today.

Parent: Help us to be kind to all.

Child: Walk with me today, dear God, in all that I do.

(Now share this blessing.)

Parent: May God walk with you today.

Child: And may God walk with you.

In the Evening

Parent: Let us take time now to thank God for our day, our joys and difficulties, our surprises and disappointments.

(Pause for a few seconds)

Child: Thank you, God, for all that is beautiful in our world.

Parent: Thank you for daylight and for your Word that lights up our hearts.

Parent/Child: We praise you, O God, for the earth and all who live on it. You love us, O God, and you do great things for us. Holy is your name. Amen.

(Now trace the sign of the cross on your child's forehead.)

We Remember and Celebrate

In the Morning

Parent: Let us rejoice today that Jesus will be with us in all we do.

Child: Thank you, Jesus, for this great gift.

Parent: Let us also remember all that Jesus has done for us.

> We proclaim your Death, O Lord, and profess your Resurrection until you come again.

Parent: We are filled with wonder and praise, O God, when we see what you have done for us through Jesus Christ, your Son.

Child: Help us to remember and celebrate. Amen.

Parent: Thank you, Jesus, for being with us always. May we walk with you this day. Amen.

In the Evening

Child: Thank you, Jesus, for being here with us.

Parent: Let us listen together to God's Word.

> Jesus said to his followers,
> "Where two or three are gathered in my name,
> I am there among them."
>
> —Matthew 18:20

Child: Help me to remember these words, dear God, tonight and always.

Parent: Bless my child as he/she prepares to receive Jesus in First Communion.

Child: Open my heart to receive Jesus, dear God.

Parent: Send your Holy Spirit to my child and to us as a family.

Parent/Child: Through Jesus, all honour and glory is yours, Almighty Father, for ever and ever. Amen.

(Now trace the sign of the cross on your child's forehead.)

We Share the Bread of Life

In the Morning

Parent: Let us remember that God has given us the sacrament of Eucharist, the gift of Jesus, who comes to us in communion and lives within us.

Child: Thank you, God, for this special sacrament.

Parent: We believe that in holy communion, we receive you, Jesus, the Bread of Life. We believe that you are the real bread come down from heaven for us. Amen.

Child: As I prepare for this sacrament, Jesus, please fill my heart with your love.

Parent: Let us listen now to the words of Jesus.

> "I am the living bread.
> Whoever eats of this bread will live forever."
> —John 6:51

Parent: May peace be in your heart as you prepare to receive Jesus.

(Now share a sign of peace.)

In the Evening

Parent: As the time draws near for your First Communion, I ask God to bless you with peace, joy, and love.

Child: Open my heart to your Law of Love, O God.

Parent: I ask God to open your heart to receive Jesus.

Child: Open my heart to Jesus, O God.

Parent: I ask God to open your heart to this message.

> Jesus is the Bread of Life
> who comes to us in communion.
> He helps us to be both good and holy.

Parent: Loving God, thank you for the gift of Jesus. Bless my child as he/she prepares to receive him in the Eucharist.

(Now trace the sign of the cross on your child's forehead.)

3 We Share God's Word

Goals

- **to help your child discover the Bible as the great story of God's love, a story that we continue to live today**
- **to awaken in your child's heart a love for Scripture**
- **to reveal to your child how God's Word speaks to us in the liturgy**

Parent/child conversations

Pages 19, 20, and 21

- Look at the "People of Faith" gallery with your child. Explain that these were some of the "faith people" who came before Jesus. Their stories are found in the Bible. Then share your own family history. Talk especially about stories that reveal the values your family holds: for example, courage in hard times, faithful love, honesty, fairness toward all, family unity, and family celebrations.
- Read your child the section on page 20 that begins with "At the time of Abraham." Explain that this is the beginning of the story of our faith in the Bible. Spend some time on God's Law of Love on page 21. Read each line of God's Law of Love on page 21, and have your child repeat it after you. End this conversation by blessing your child, saying, "May you always live God's Law of Love, and may I live it, too." Your child answers, "Amen."

Pages 22, 23, and 24

- Read about David, Isaiah, and John the Baptist on page 22. Has your child heard of any of them before? What does he or she remember?
- Explain that King David wrote many of the psalms in the Bible. Every Sunday at Mass, we sing a psalm such as this one:

> Praise the Lord, all you nations!
> Praise God, all people everywhere.
> For great is God's love for us,
> and this love lasts forever.
> Praise the Lord!
>
> —adapted from Psalm 117

- Share with your child that sometimes the first reading at Mass is from the prophet Isaiah. Together, read Isaiah's message on page 22.
- Also share the message from John the Baptist on page 22. Like Isaiah, John was a prophet, someone who spoke for God. He announced the coming of Jesus. John was also the cousin of Jesus.
- Read pages 23 and 24 ahead of time so you can tell the story in your own words. End by saying, "And the story continues." Ask how your child might help Jesus continue the great story of God's love.

Pages 25, 26, and 27

- After reading together the paragraph at the beginning of page 25, talk about the three readings at Mass. God's Word teaches us how to follow Jesus in all that we do. How can God's Word help your family make decisions, give thanks, and forgive others?
- Practise the response we say at the end of the first and second readings ("Thanks be to God") on page 25, and after the gospel ("Praise to you, Lord Jesus Christ") on page 26.
- Explain that the Apostles' Creed (on page 27), which we pray at Mass, contains the basic teachings of our faith. Pray parts of it and have your child repeat the words after you.

Pages 28 and 29

- Go over the "Did You Know?" questions on page 28 with your child. Talk about the people or things your child could pray for during the intercessory prayers. Share who and what you pray for as well. Practise the response to these prayers: "Lord, hear our prayer."
- Finish the sentences on page 29, then discuss the answers with your child. Review the "Words to Remember." Be sure your child can define them in his or her own words. End by praying the words "From the Liturgy."

4 We Give Thanks

Goals

- **to help your child discover that thanksgiving is at the heart of the Eucharist and of our Christian lives**
- **to help your child understand the meaning of sharing bread and wine**
- **to reaffirm your child's desire to give thanks to God and show gratitude to others**

Family conversations

Pages **30 and 31**

- Read together the story of Alicia and Kieran on page 30. Talk about how bread is made and remember times when you have eaten delicious bread.
- Help your child see the connection between this story and sharing the bread and wine at Mass, described on page 31. For example, we come together to share the Bread of Life; we give thanks and praise; we ask God to change us, just as wheat changes into bread.

Pages **32, 33, and 34**

- Read together the "Blessed are you" prayers on page 32. Then invite your child to respond to the "What Do You Think?" questions.
- Practise together the prayers and responses on page 33.
- Explain the "Thank-you Game" to your child. If possible, involve your entire family in this exercise.

- Talk to your child about how he or she decorated the prayer on page 34, then pray it together slowly.

Pages **35, 36, and 37**

- Does your child remember praying the Holy, Holy, Holy prayer, on page 35, at Mass? Help him or her memorize the first two lines.
- Go over the "Did You Know?" statements on page 35. Remind your child that he or she is also "blessed" and loved by God.
- Share the thanksgiving prayer on page 36 with your child.
- Review the sentences at the top of page 37. Help your child fill in the missing words and unscramble the three mixed-up words. Review the "Words to Remember." Be sure your child can define them in his or her own words. End by praying the words "From the Liturgy."

Goals

- **to teach your child the importance of remembering Jesus, in daily life and at Mass**
- **to help your child become more familiar with the Eucharistic Prayer, the great prayer of thanksgiving at Mass**
- **to strengthen in your child's heart the desire to receive Jesus at First Communion**

Parent/child conversations

Pages 38, 39, and 40

- Talk about the things your child remembers most about family celebrations. Share with him or her that the Mass is a great celebration: every week, we are invited to gather, remember, and celebrate the things Jesus did and said when he lived on earth.
- Read the three priest's statements in red on pages 39 and 40, and read the reply in blue on page 40. These three statements express what the Church calls the Paschal mystery, which is at the heart of our faith. Talk about the illustrations and how everything is centred on Jesus.

Pages 41, 42, and 43

- Read the text at the top of page 41. Ask your child if he or she knows what "sacrifice" means. Then explain it in your own words. Share Alex's story (page 42) together.
- Discuss the "What Do You Think?" questions on page 43. Does your child remember ever sacrificing something? Talk about a time when you sacrificed something for someone you love.

Pages 44, 45, 46, and 47

- Read pages 45 to 46, and share with your child how we pray for people all over the world at every Mass. We pray for the living and the dead. We pray to Mary and the saints. We conclude all these prayers by singing the Great Amen on page 46. Explain that when we say "Amen," we are saying we believe.
- Talk about the young people in the illustration on page 45. Why do they look happy? What might they be thinking?
- Review what your child wrote on page 46 and talk about it together.
- Help your child match the two columns on page 47. Talk about what each phrase means.
- Together do the prayer exercise in or near your child's prayer corner. Have your child light the candle as you share this experience.

6 We Share the Bread of Life

Goals

- to help your child better understand the concept of being in communion with someone
- to help your child focus on the sacraments of baptism and Eucharist
- to deepen your child's desire to be in communion with Jesus

Parent/child conversations

Pages 48 and 49

- Together, read Trinh's story. How does she remember her mother? How does her mother remember her? Explain that remembering someone keeps us "in communion" with that person.
- Review the prayer in "From the Liturgy" on page 49. Make the connection between Trinh and her mother staying "in communion" and Christians staying in communion with Jesus.

Pages 50 and 51

- Talk about your child's baptism. Explain that this was his or her first sacrament. Share your memories of that day.
- Read "Jesus is the Real Bread" on page 51. Explain that Jesus gave bread to hungry people and called himself the bread of life. God gives us spiritual food to help us be good and holy, as Jesus was.

Pages 52, 53, 54, and 55

- Pray the Lord's Prayer (the Our Father) together. Your child has probably memorized it by now. If not, practise it together.

- Explain that we make peace with one another before we receive Jesus in communion. Offer each other a sign of peace, as on page 52.
- Read together the first section on page 54.

Page 55

- Review the questions and your child's answers.
- Read the "Did You Know?" statement together. Be sure your child can explain the "Words to Remember" in his or her own words.
- Before closing, offer your child this blessing with your hands on his or her head: *"May God bless you as you prepare to receive your First Communion. God loves you very much, and I do, too!"*

Conclusion

Congratulations! You have journeyed with your child to his or her First Communion. May you both continue to talk and pray and share in the Eucharist together long after this happy celebration.

This Family Guide is an integral part of *We Share in the Eucharist—Child's Book.*

© 2010 Novalis Publishing Inc.,

Authors: Francoise Darcy-Berube and Jean-Paul Berube
Editors, New Edition: Gwen Costello and Myrtle Power
Cover: Anna Payne-Krzyzanowski
Design & Layout: Sarah Orr, ArtPlus
Photo credits: Page 3: © iStockphoto.com/bobbieo; Page 4: © WP Wittman Photography; Page 5: © iStockphoto.com/ Legacy One Photography; Page 14: © WP Wittman Photography.
Illustrations: June Bradford: p. 6; Suzanne Mogensen: p. 15.

NOVALIS
10 Lower Spadina Ave., Suite 400,
Toronto, ON, Canada M5V 2Z2
www.novalis.ca

Published in the United States by
Twenty-Third Publications
P.O. Box 6015, New London, CT. 06320
www.23rdpublications.com

We Lift Our Hearts

After the prayers offering the bread and wine, the priest asks us to pray with him.

The Lord be with you.

All answer:

And with your spirit.

Lift up your hearts.

All answer:

We lift them up to the Lord.

Let us give thanks to the Lord our God.

All answer:

It is right and just.

Do you know what it means to "give thanks" at Mass? It means praising God with love and gratitude. The word **Eucharist** means "thanksgiving." Mass is a great thanksgiving celebration!

The Thank-you Game

Do you always remember to say thank you?

To help you remember, try playing a Thank-you game with your family or friends.

For three days, all players try to notice and count the number of times in a day that they say "thank you" in a kind way.

At the end of day 3, talk about your thank yous and decide who won.

33

We Begin the "Great Prayer"

You have already learned that the word **Eucharist** means "thanksgiving." The most important part of the Liturgy of the Eucharist is the great prayer of thanksgiving, which is called the **Eucharistic Prayer**.

The priest leads up to the Eucharistic Prayer by praising God for giving us life, our beautiful universe, and the joy and love we share with one another.

Read this prayer slowly and then decorate it by drawing some of the things it mentions.

We thank you for all that is beautiful in the world
and for the happiness you have given us.

We praise you for daylight and for your word,
which lights up our minds.

We praise you for the earth,
for all the people who live on it,
and for our life, which comes from you.

We know that you are good.
You love us and do great things for us.

Let Us Pray

Think about some of the wonderful things in your life. Then, with all your heart, mind, and voice, say this beautiful prayer of praise:

Holy, Holy,
Holy Lord God of hosts.
Heaven and earth
are full of your glory.
Hosanna
in the highest.

Blessed is he who comes
in the name of the Lord.
Hosanna
in the highest.

Did You Know?

Holy is the word that describes perfect goodness and love.

Glory is the praise we give to great beauty or majesty like **God's.**

Hosanna is a shout of joy from the Hebrew language.

Blessed means holy, great, and loved by God.

Do you sometimes give thanks to God during the day? For what are you most grateful? What words do you use? Do you use your prayer corner sometimes? Remember, it is your very own space for praising and thanking God.

We Can Pray Always

At any moment in the day, somewhere in the world, Mass is being celebrated. The most beautiful prayer you can say any time of the day is a thanksgiving prayer, like the Eucharistic Prayer at Mass.

It only takes a minute and you will be together with Christians all over the world. Here is how you can do it.

✝ Stretch your body until you feel relaxed.

✝ Stand straight on both feet. Close your eyes.

Remember that you are standing on our beautiful planet Earth!

✝ Breathe deeply two or three times.

Remember that God is looking at you with love.

MAY YOUR KINGDOM COME!

Then pray this way:

Dear God, here I am,
giving thanks for this day.
With Jesus your Son,
I offer you praise.
I give you my love
and all that I do!
Amen.

The Church Teaches...

It is always possible to pray. In fact, we NEED to pray.

—adapted for children from CCC #2757

Fill in the missing words.

1. **We give thanks to the Father with J_____.**

2. **We carry b_____ and wine in the Presentation of the _____.**

3. **The priest says, "The L_____ be with y___."**

4. **We answer, "A___ with y____ spirit."**

5. **The word "Eucharist" means "t_____."**

6. **At Mass we say t_____ y___ to God.**

We use these words of praise at Mass. Can you read them?

HINT: start at the end.

YLOH   DESSELB   ANNASOH

....

....

....

Words to Remember...

Prayer ~ talking with God

Prayer corner ~ your very own place to pray

Eucharistic Prayer ~ the "great prayer" of the Mass

Glory ~ the kind of praise we give to God

From the Liturgy

We know that you are good, O God. You love us and do great things for us.

—Eucharistic Prayer I for Children

Most of us like to remember and celebrate the important days in our lives.

On the day of your First Communion, your family will remember the great joy they felt when you were born. They want this day to be very special for you and they will celebrate it with you.

At Mass we celebrate Jesus! We remember his last meal, his death, and his resurrection. We remember that he loved and served others.

We remember that he promised to be with us always.

At Mass, the priest repeats the words of Jesus from the Last Supper. He takes the bread in his hands and says, as Jesus said:

Take this, all of you, and eat of it, for this is my Body, which will be given up for you.

Then the priest takes the cup of wine and says, as Jesus said:

Take this, all of you, and drink from it, for this is the chalice of my Blood.

After each of these invitations, the priest shows us the bread, then the wine, which have become the presence of the risen Jesus among us.

We "See" with Faith

At the Last Supper, the apostles saw Jesus with their own eyes. At Mass we do not see him. But we believe that he is with us. That is why the priest invites us to proclaim our faith.

The priest says:

The mystery of faith.

All reply with great joy:

We proclaim your Death, O Lord, and profess your Resurrection until you come again.

The Church Teaches...

Jesus himself is with us, though we can't see him, at every Eucharistic celebration.

—adapted for children from CCC #1348

Can you finish these sentences?

✧ Jesus died on the C__ __ __ __.

✧ God r__ __ __ __ __ Jesus from the dead.

✧ J__ __ __ __ will come again.

We Imitate Jesus

After giving them the bread and the wine, Jesus told his friends: "Do this in memory of me." At Mass we celebrate in memory of him. But remembering Jesus also means following him on the path to God's love.

When we do something that is difficult for us, we call it a **sacrifice**. And when we sacrifice for someone else, we are following Jesus.

Can you remember a sacrifice you made for someone? In the frame on this page, draw a picture of what you did.

Alex Makes a Sacrifice

Five whole days. I can't stand it!

Here's how Alex made a sacrifice for someone. Alex's best friend, Sam, broke his arm. He had to stay home from school for five days.

Meanwhile, Alex had just received a fun invitation.

Mom, the Riveras invited me to go skating this afternoon. Can I go, please?

Sure you can. I'll make you a snack to take.

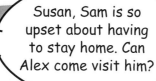

Susan, Sam is so upset about having to stay home. Can Alex come visit him?

Alex has just been invited to go skating, but I'll talk to him about it.

If I go over to Sam's, I won't be able to go skating.

That's true. You won't.

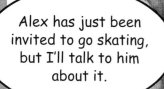

42

But if I don't visit Sam, he'll be very lonely.

Okay, I'll go see Sam. I can go skating some other time. I'll go tell the Riveras.

Hey, Sam. I brought a new game we can play.

Boy, am I glad to see you!

From the Bible

People will know you are my followers when you show love for one another.

—adapted from John 13:35

What Do You Think?

1. **What was Alex's sacrifice?**

....

2. **Do you think it was difficult for Alex to give up going skating?**

....

3. **Why do you think Alex did it?**

....

We Pray Together

Every week at Mass, we celebrate with others in our parish because Jesus is with us. We sing together, pray together, and share the Lord's Supper. We need one another. Together we try to follow the path to God.

During the Eucharistic Prayer, we pray for one another and for people all over the world. Here's what the priest says in our name:

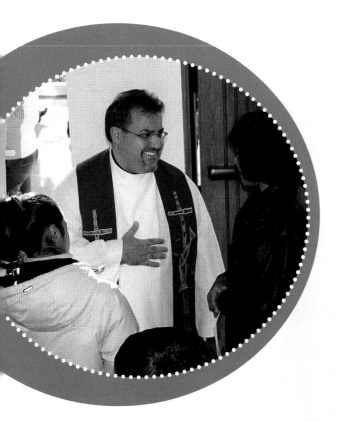

Father, because you love us, you invite us to come to your table. Fill us with the joy of the Holy Spirit as we receive the body and blood of your Son.

Lord, you never forget any of your children. We ask you to take care of those we love, especially of _____ and _____, and we pray for those who have died.

Remember everyone who is suffering from pain or sorrow. Remember Christians everywhere and all other people in the world.

We are filled with wonder and praise when we see what you do for us through Jesus your Son.

Did you notice that in this prayer we pray for those who have died? That's because we believe that when we die, we go to God.

We also believe that the people in heaven pray for us.

At Mass we pray:

Gather us all together into your kingdom.
There we will be happy for ever
with the Virgin Mary,
Mother of God and our mother.
There all the friends of Jesus the Lord
will sing a song of joy.

—Eucharistic Prayer II
for Children

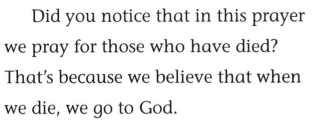

We Offer Ourselves

We began the great prayer of the Eucharist by offering bread and wine to God. Through the Holy Spirit, these gifts became the presence of the risen Lord.

Now, at the end of this great prayer, we offer *ourselves* with Jesus. The priest prays:

Through him, and with him, and in him,
O God, almighty Father,
in the unity of the Holy Spirit,
all glory and honour is yours, for ever and ever.
All sing the great Amen.
Amen!
Amen, yes, I believe,
Amen, Amen, Amen!

Every person gathered at Mass is saying yes to Jesus. Yes, Jesus, we believe you are here with us. Yes, we want to be one with you.

When you sing the great Amen, what is in your mind and heart?

Write your thoughts in the empty bubble in the picture on this page.

Try to match these two columns. Draw a line to the correct answer.

1. The last meal of Jesus	The great prayer of thanksgiving
2. Presentation of the Gifts	We say yes to our faith
3. Offertory collection (part of Preparation of the Gifts)	We contribute our own money
4. Sacrifice	The Last Supper
5. Eucharistic Prayer	We carry the bread and wine
6. Great Amen	We do something difficult for someone

Spend time at prayer thinking about Jesus and how he is always with you. At Mass, this is what we remember and celebrate. Here is how you can talk to Jesus about this:

✝ Sit down in your special prayer corner.

✝ Close your eyes.

✝ Breathe slowly and deeply a few times until you feel quiet inside.

✝ In a very soft voice or in your heart, slowly say a short prayer from the Mass: for example, "Holy, holy, holy" or "Blessed are you" or "Amen."

✝ Say it over and over, as often as you like, until the peace of God fills your heart.

✝ Now share with Jesus whatever is in your heart.

✝ End your prayer time with these words: "Through Jesus, all glory and honour is yours, almighty Father, for ever and ever. Amen."

From the Bible

My father and I will come to you and make our home with you.

—adapted from John 14:23

47

Did You Know?

▸ **We can be in communion with those around us.**

▸ **We can be in communion in spirit—as we are with Jesus.**

▸ **We can be in communion even with someone who is far away from us.**

Very soon you will celebrate your First Communion! The word **communion** means "being together," but it means even more than that. It means "being together in love."

When we share the Bread of Life, we are in communion with Jesus.

• • • • • •

Trinh's mother was going to London for a business trip. She was going to be gone for a week. Trinh didn't want her mother to miss her. When her mom was not looking, Trinh put a picture of herself in her mom's suitcase.

When Trinh's mother arrived at her hotel room, she opened her suitcase. She found Trinh's picture and put it on the table next to her bed. She was so happy to see Trinh's smiling face there beside her.

Trinh understood that even though her mother was travelling, they still could be together. They still could be "in communion."

From the Liturgy

Send the Holy Spirit to all of us who share in this meal. May this Spirit bring us closer together in the family of the Church.

—Eucharistic Prayer II
for Children

When people really love and understand one another as Trinh and her mother do, they are in communion. When they share hopes and dreams and work together, they are in communion.

We Celebrate Sacraments

The Church has very special celebrations called **sacraments** that keep us in communion with God and one another. The sacraments are signs of love from Jesus.

Can you fill in the names of these sacraments?

In b_____, Jesus tells us through the sign of water:

"God my Father loves you. You are God's own child."

In H_____ C_____, Jesus tells us through the signs of bread and wine:

"I am the Living Bread. Whoever eats this bread will have life forever."

By calling us God's children in baptism and giving himself to us in Communion, Jesus is saying, "I am with you always."

Jesus Is the Real Bread

One day, five thousand people followed Jesus up a mountain to learn more about God. They were very happy to hear Jesus' message, but by lunchtime they were all hungry. There was no market nearby, but a child had five small loaves of bread and two fish. He gladly gave them to Jesus.

With these gifts Jesus did a wonderful thing.

He took the loaves of bread and the fish and gave thanks to God. Then his followers shared this food with the crowd. Everyone had enough to eat.

The next day, the people came back again. At lunchtime they said: "We are hungry. Give us more bread."

Here is what Jesus said to them: "The 'real bread' comes down from heaven as a gift from God. I am the Living Bread, the real bread. All those who eat this bread will live forever."

The Church Teaches...

Holy Communion unites us more closely to Christ.

—adapted for children from CCC #1391

Jesus was telling them that God feeds us in two ways. God gives us food to feed our bodies and God gives us spiritual food to help us become good and holy.

Jesus is the Bread of Life who comes to us in Communion. He helps us to be good and holy.

We Prepare for Communion

At Mass, before sharing the Bread of Life, we say together the Lord's Prayer, the prayer Jesus taught us. When we pray this prayer, we say that we want to live in communion with God and others. Pray it often at home with your family.

The Lord's Prayer

Our Father, who art in heaven,
hallowed be thy name,
thy kingdom come, thy will be done
on earth as it is in heaven.

Give us this day our daily bread,
and forgive us our trespasses,
as we forgive those who trespass against us;
and lead us not into temptation,
but deliver us from evil. Amen.

Next, we make peace with one another.

Sometimes arguments and disagreements keep us apart, and we find it hard to make peace. But Jesus is with us to help us share peace.

That is why the priest tells us:

The peace of the Lord be with you always.

And all answer:

And with your spirit.

Then we offer one another a sign of peace. We say:

Peace be with you.
or
The peace of Christ be with you.

We Ask for Mercy

Maybe there is someone you would like to make peace with, but this person is not present. Maybe you never had the chance to say "sorry."

This point in the Mass is a time to ask God to forgive us for anything we forgot about. We have a time to ask for forgiveness for anything we may have done to hurt others.

Lamb of God, you take away the sins of the world, have mercy on us.

Lamb of God, you take away the sins of the world, have mercy on us.

Lamb of God, you take away the sins of the world, grant us peace.

Lamb of God is one of the special names the Church uses for Jesus.

We Are One with Jesus

Now comes the great moment you are preparing for. The people go towards the altar to receive Holy Communion. Soon you will be able to do this, too.

The priest holds up the bread and says: **The Body of Christ.**

The people bow slightly and put forward their cupped hands. As they receive the host in their hand, each person answers: **Amen.**

Then they put the host in their mouth.

The priest might also offer the wine, saying: **The Blood of Christ.**

People bow slightly and reach for the chalice. Each answers: **Amen.**

Then they take a sip from the cup.

Now the Mass is drawing to a close.

The priest or deacon turns to the people and says:

Go forth, the Mass is ended.

All answer: **Thanks be to God!**

Remember, when you leave the church, Jesus goes with you. He walks with you always in all that you do.

Did You Know?

When you receive your First Communion, with your eyes, you will see only the bread and wine. With your mouth, you will taste only the bread and wine. But in your heart, you will know that the Risen Christ is within you and will help you live in communion with him and with others.

Congratulations! Soon you will meet the Lord Jesus in Holy Communion for the first time! You can then join your parish community every Sunday and receive Jesus, the Bread of Life.

✦ What are some ways you can love and serve the Lord at home, at school, and everywhere you go?

....

....

....

Words to Remember...

Communion ~ being together in love

Sacraments ~ signs of love and communion that Jesus gave us

Lamb of God ~ a special church name for Jesus

Amen ~ yes, I do believe!

Let Us Pray

How would you finish this prayer?

Dear God, thank you for my First Communion Day...

....

....

Prayers to Remember

In this book you have learned about the Mass and the prayers we pray at Mass. You will find some of these prayers in *My Prayer Book,* which starts on the next page. You might want to learn some of these prayers by heart. Pray them at home in your prayer corner. Pray them joyfully at Mass. Pray them every day wherever you are!

How to make your very own prayer book
You will need:

✧ scissors

✧ ribbon, string, wool, or staples to
  hold your book together

✧ a marker or coloured pencil

To make your prayer book:

✧ Cut out the pages of *My Prayer Book* with scissors.

✧ Fold each page in half.

✧ Use ribbon, string, wool, or staples
  to hold your book together.

✧ Write your name in marker or coloured
  pencil in your prayer book.

My Prayer Book

Jesus,
you are
the bread of life.

Praise to you, Lord Jesus Christ!

This book belongs to

. . . .

May the grace of our Lord Jesus Christ be with me always.

Apostles' Creed

I believe in God, the Father almighty,
Creator of heaven and earth, and in
Jesus Christ, his only Son, our Lord,
  who was conceived by the Holy Spirit,
  born of the Virgin Mary,
  suffered under Pontius Pilate,
  was crucified, died and was buried;
  he descended into hell;
  on the third day he rose again from
  the dead;
  he ascended into heaven,
  and is seated at the right hand of
  God the Father almighty;
  from there he will come to judge
  the living and the dead.
I believe in the Holy Spirit,
  the holy catholic Church,
  the communion of saints,
  the forgiveness of sins,
  the resurrection of the body,
  and life everlasting.
Amen.

The Sign of the Cross

In the name of the Father,
and of the Son,
and of the Holy Spirit.
Amen.

Come, Holy Spirit

Come, Holy Spirit,
fill the hearts of your faithful
and kindle in them
the fire of your love.
Send forth your Spirit, O Lord,
and renew the face of the earth.
Amen.

Lord, Hear My Prayer

Lord, have mercy.
Christ, have mercy.
Lord, have mercy.

The Peace Prayer of St. Francis

Lord, make me an instrument of your peace.
Where there is hatred, let me sow love;
where there is injury, pardon;
where there is doubt, faith;
where there is despair, hope;
where there is darkness, light;
where there is sadness, joy.
Divine Master, grant that I may not so much seek
to be consoled, as to console;
to be understood as to understand;
to be loved as to love.
For it is in giving that we receive;
it is in pardoning that we are pardoned;
and it is in dying that we are born to eternal life.
Amen.

Grace before Meals

Bless us, O Lord,
and these your gifts
which we are about to receive
from your goodness.
Through Christ our Lord.
Amen.

Glory to God

Glory to God in the highest,
and on earth peace to people of good will.
We praise you, we bless you,
we adore you, we glorify you,
we give you thanks for your great glory,
Lord God, heavenly King,
O God, almighty Father.
Amen.

Hosanna in the Highest

Holy, Holy,
Holy Lord God of hosts.

Glory Be

Glory to the Father,
and to the Son,
and to the Holy Spirit.
As it was in the beginning,
is now,
and will be forever.
Amen.

Hail Mary

Hail Mary, full of grace,
the Lord is with you.
Blessed are you among women
and blessed is the fruit of your womb,
Jesus.
Holy Mary,
Mother of God,
pray for us sinners,
now
and at the hour of our death.
Amen.

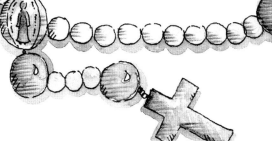

Blessed are you,
Lord God of all creation.

Prayer of St. Clare of Assisi

Blessed are you, my Lord God,
for creating me and giving me life;
and by your death on the cross,
blessed are you, Jesus, for redeeming me
and giving me eternal life.
Amen.

Memorial Acclamation

We proclaim your Death, O Lord,
and profess your Resurrection
until you come again.

The Lord's Prayer
Our Father

Our Father,
who art in heaven,
hallowed be thy name,
thy kingdom come,
thy will be done
on earth
as it is in heaven.

Give us this day
our daily bread,
and forgive us our trespasses,
as we forgive those
who trespass against us;
and lead us not into temptation,
but deliver us from evil.
Amen.